Ephesians
Blessed!

Linda Osborne

Copyright © 2014 Linda Osborne

Published by Catch the Vision! Press

504 A Harbor View Drive, Klamath Falls, OR 97601

All rights reserved.

ISBN-10: 0615948839
ISBN-13: 978-0615948836

CONTENTS

	Preface	1
1	Ephesians 1	3
2	Ephesians 2	15
3	Ephesians 3	27
4	Ephesians 4	39
5	Ephesians 5	51
6	Ephesians 6	63
	About the Author	75

PREFACE

The letter to the Ephesians is one of the four letters known as the Prison Epistles, written by the apostle Paul during his first imprisonment in Rome. Three of these epistles—Ephesians, Colossians and Philemon were written at the same time, approximately 60 AD, and delivered by the same man, Tychicus.

Paul's history with the Ephesian church is important. He first stopped in Ephesus on his way back to Antioch from his second missionary journey. On his third missionary journey, he stayed in Ephesus for approximately three years. After finishing the remainder of his journey, on his return to Jerusalem, Paul called the elders of the Ephesian church to meet with him in Miletus, in order to say his farewells. Acts 20:36-38 gives us a sense of the affection that had grown between Paul and the Ephesians: "And when he had said these things, he knelt down and prayed with them all. And they began to weep aloud and embraced Paul, and repeatedly kissed him, grieving especially over the word which he had spoken, that they should see his face no more."

Now, almost ten years after his original meeting with them, he writes to this beloved church. We notice this letter is general in nature, rather than specific, and without personal messages or greetings. It is presumed that this is because, although the letter was originally sent to the Ephesians, it was written as a Christian treatise, to be sent throughout the Asian area and read by all the churches there.

There are different schools of thought on the theme of Ephesians. The believers' riches in Christ is a predominant point—especially seeing that the first three chapters deal with this wonderful subject. But equally significant is the theme of the building of the body of Christ, found in chapter 4. Chapters 1-3 give us the position and privileges of the Christian; chapters 4-6, the practice and responsibilities of the Christian.

Have you ever heard of someone who died in the midst of great poverty, only to be discovered to have been very, very wealthy? Some of us live our Christian lives just like this—looking like spiritual paupers: weak, powerless, and ineffective, while all the time we have a spiritual bank account that reveals that we are rich! As you study chapter one of the letter to the Ephesians, make note of all that you, as a Christian, have in your heavenly bank account: adoption, acceptance, redemption, forgiveness, wisdom, inheritance, the seal of the Holy Spirit, life, grace, and citizenship—every spiritual blessing in the heavenly places in Christ (Ephesians 1:3)!

EPHESIANS 1

Day 1
Daily Facts

Read Ephesians 1:1-3

Be sure to begin your study today and every day with a word of prayer. The great desire of your heart should be that the Holy Spirit would guide you into all the truth and apply that truth to your life personally.

All the spiritual blessings:
We might remember that it has been said that Ephesians and Colossians are twin epistles. In both letters, Paul addresses himself by the title "apostle." Paul was an apostle of Jesus Christ: a special messenger or *sent one*. Paul was one of the unique group of men chosen by God to minister to the church at its foundation—teaching, preaching, praying, and building up the body of Christ, as well as writing the books and letters which would complete the Word of God.

Paul, as an apostle, was a man of great authority in the church and was able to write to the Ephesians from this strong position. And yet, Paul himself was a mere man and has left us with an example of great humility.

1. Look at these words of Paul in which he describes himself. What does he say?

   1 Corinthians 15:8-9

   2 Corinthians 12:11

   Ephesians 3:8

   1 Timothy 1:15

   a. What can you learn by balancing the great strength and authority of Paul's position with his great humility as a sinner saved by grace?

After a word of double blessing to the believers at Ephesus, in verse 3 Paul begins to paint the magnificent portrait of spiritual blessings planned and given by God to believers in Christ.

2. What blessings has God provided for the believer in Christ? v. 3

   a. According to this verse, is there anything of a spiritual nature that God has not provided for us?

One commentator speaks of these spiritual blessings as "every spiritual enrichment needed for the spiritual life."

   b. Is this bestowment of blessing something that has already happened or is it something that will happen in the future?

   c. Sometimes we find ourselves asking for things that are already ours. Do we need to ask God to give us these spiritual blessings? What should we do?

3. The following verses reveal some of the spiritual blessings that are ours in Christ. Look them up, and as you think about them, consider whether or not it is necessary for us to ask God to give us these blessings.

   Love—Romans 5:5

   Peace—John 14:27

   Joy—John 15:11

   Strength—Philippians 4:13

   a. What does 2 Peter 1:3 tell us about the blessings the Father has given us?

4. From Ephesians 1:3:

   ✤ From where do our spiritual blessings emanate?

John MacArthur says this encompasses the entire supernatural realm of God, His complete domain, the full extent of His divine operation.

   ✤ In whom are these blessings ours?

The words in Christ are key to this entire passage. In union with Christ we possess every spiritual blessing in the heavenly places. In his commentary on Ephesians, John MacArthur gives us a sense of the riches that are ours in Christ:

   Christ's riches are our riches,
   Christ's resources are our resources,
   Christ's righteousness is our righteousness,

Christ's power is our power,
Christ's position is our position,
Christ's privilege is our privilege,
Christ's possessions are our possessions,
His practice is our practice;
Where He is, we are; what He is, we are;
What He has, we have; what He does, we do ...

Stone of Remembrance:

"Blessed be the God and Father of our Lord Jesus Christ, who has blessed us with every spiritual blessing in the heavenly places in Christ." Ephesians 1:3

Day 2
Daily Facts
Read Ephesians 1:3-14

Spiritual blessings enumerated:
As we begin today to look individually at some of the spiritual blessings bestowed on us in Christ, we begin again in verse 3.

1. *Who* has blessed us with every spiritual blessing, according to verse 3?

The next 11 verses (4-14), which reveal these blessings, are broken up into three sections. We will see in these verses that all three Persons of the Trinity are involved in our salvation.

Blessings from the Father (v. 4-6):
2. In verse 4 we're given the first of many blessings. From this verse:

✣ What did God do?

✠ When did He do it?
✠ Why did He do it?

Verse 4 in the Amplified says that "He ... actually picked us out for Himself as His own."

    a. Verse 5 gives us the second blessing. Again:

✠ What did God do?
✠ Why did He do it?

The concept of election and predestination are difficult concepts for us to understand. Warren Wiersbe says that the word predestination, as it is used in the Bible, refers primarily to what God does for *saved* people. "Nowhere in the Bible are we taught that people are predestined to Hell, because this word refers only to God's people."

    b. As God's people, we were predestined to adoption as sons. Romans 8:15-17 is a wonderful passage with this thought in mind. What does it teach you?

Verse 6 gives us another blessing of God the Father. NKJV puts it this way: "... to the praise of the glory of His grace, by which He has made us accepted in the Beloved."

    c. What does it mean to you that you are *accepted in the Beloved?* (Concentrate on the word *accepted*.)

Blessings from the Son (v. 7-12):
3. In verse 7, we see two blessings of God the Son. What are they?

a. The word *redeemed* means paying a ransom in order to release a person from bondage. With what did Jesus redeem you? 1 Peter 1:18-19

b. What does this fact say to you about the love of your Savior?

c. Verse 7 in the Amplified speaks of the "remission (forgiveness) of our offenses (shortcomings and trespasses)." Share what it means to know you are forgiven. (This is huge!)

In verses 8-10, we see that Jesus has revealed God's will to us. These verses take us forward to a day not far in the future when all things will be "summed up" in Christ. This passage speaks of the completion of history, when the millennial kingdom will begin.

d. What will take place at that time according to Philippians 2:10-11?

In verses 11-12, we see that in Jesus we have obtained an inheritance. As we examine these aspects of our salvation, we see this is one which is primarily future—we will receive our completed inheritance in the ages to come.

e. What does Romans 8:17 say about this?

The Amplified says, "In Him we also were made (God's) heritage (portion) and we obtained an inheritance."

LESSON ONE

This reveals that not only are we promised to share in the inheritance of Jesus, but we are *His* inheritance!

Blessings from the Holy Spirit (v. 13-14):
4. What is the primary work of the Holy Spirit in regard to our salvation? v. 13

   a. What does verse 14 tell us about the Holy Spirit?

The Holy Spirit gives us the security that we will one day be fully redeemed and receive our inheritance in Christ!

   b. Go back over what you have seen in these verses today, and share which of these blessings means the most to you personally.

Review this week's memory verse.

Day 3
Daily Facts

Read Ephesians 1:15-23

Paul's prayer for the Ephesians:
As Paul moves on from the presentation of the glorious riches of Christ that belong to every believer, he turns his thoughts from God and all He has done for us in Christ, to the Ephesian believers themselves.

EPHESIANS: BLESSED!

1. What does Paul say he has *heard* of the Ephesians? v. 15

    a. What two things does Paul *do* for them? v. 16

2. Paul begins his prayer by asking the Lord to give them two things. What are they? v. 17

The Amplified says, "That He may give you a spirit of wisdom and revelation (of insight into mysteries and secrets) in the (deep and intimate) knowledge of Him."

   a. How is it that we get to know God and His will?

   b. Do you see that this is something that you can pray for yourself as you open God's Word? What kind of a difference might this make?

   c. Is there anyone you would like to pray this prayer for?

Secondarily, Paul prays that the eyes of their heart may be enlightened. The Amplified says, "By having the eyes of your heart flooded with light so that you may know and understand …"

3. Read 1 Corinthians 2:9-16 and share how it is that we receive spiritual truths.

There are three things that Paul prays for the Ephesians to know about God:

✤ *What is the hope of His calling ...*

4. 2 Timothy 1:9 speaks of His calling. What kind of freedom does this verse give you in regard to works? Does this help you?

   a. What promise does Romans 11:29 give you?

✤ *What are the riches of the glory of His inheritance in the saints ...* (This is one of those amazing truths! We are His inheritance!)

5. Look back at Ephesians 1:6, 12, and 14 and share what you learn in these verses.

✤ *What is the surpassing greatness of His power toward us who believe ...* (Another amazing verse! Paul wants us to know the great power of God available to us who believe!)

6. What example of power is given by Paul in verse 20?

This is the power that Paul is speaking of here. The same *dunamis* (dynamite) power that raised Jesus from the dead! According to this verse, resurrection power is ours in Christ!

   a. From Acts 1:8a, from where do we get this power?

   b. Because of or according to this power:

   ✤ Do you as a Christian have power to face and overcome temptation?

✣ Do you as a Christian have the power to overcome a sinful habit?

✣ Do you as a Christian have the power to step out and witness for Christ?

✣ In which of these areas do you need power today? Claim it (stand in faith believing it is yours) in the name of Jesus Christ, according to the surpassing greatness of His power toward us who believe!

In verses 20-23, we see what God has done for Christ: He has raised Him from the dead; He has seated Him at His right hand in heavenly places; He put all things in subjection under His feet; He gave Him as head over all things to the church which is His body, the fullness of Him who fills all in all.

Christ is everything! He fills all in all. Thank God today for all that He has done for you and given you in His Son Jesus Christ. Begin to appropriate by faith what is yours. Don't ever forget the greatness of His power toward *you*—that is where you must look each and every time you need power to overcome as you live in this world!

Review this week's memory verse.

Day 4
Overview of Ephesians 1

Today we will be looking at the passage we have studied this week as a whole. The goal is to find the main lessons the Lord has for us from this chapter. Don't worry about being clever or profound—just do your best!

LESSON ONE

Find the Facts...

1. See if you can state the *content* of this week's passage in a couple of sentences. (Who is speaking, what is taking place, what is the main subject?)

Look for the Heart...

2. What do you think is the main *lesson* of this chapter? (What spiritual truths are taught here? Look for a command, a word of exhortation, a promise, etc.)

Hear Him Speak...

3. Look for a *personal application* from the content of this chapter. It should come from the lesson you got from the chapter (question 2). How will you apply the lesson to yourself?

4. Was there a particular verse that ministered to you this week? What was it and how did it minister to you?

5. Write out your stone of remembrance *from memory*!

EPHESIANS 2

Day 1
Daily Facts
Read Ephesians 2:1-7

What an incredible chapter this is. The first few words reveal all we need to know about ourselves apart from Christ—we were dead. We may have walked and we may have talked, but apart from Christ we were spiritually lifeless—like a corpse, where God was concerned, with no ability to communicate with our Maker. We needed the touch of life—and He gave it!

From death to life!
Rather than being a series of several sentences, verses 1-7 in the Greek is one long sentence—the subject of which is God, the object of which is us.

1. What fact does verse 1 tell us about ourselves?

    a. The Amplified says we were "slain" by our trespasses and sins. How does Romans 6:23a agree with this thought?

    b. Paul says we formerly walked (habitually) in sin. In case we might not be willing to agree with this assessment, see what the following verses say:

Romans 3:10

Romans 3:23

2. In verses 2-3, Paul reveals three aspects of our *previous* condition. Look carefully at these verses and see if you can explain or even personalize the ways Paul says you and I formerly lived:

   ✣ according to the course of this world ...

   ✣ according to the prince of the power of the air .

   ✣ according to the lusts of our flesh ... and our mind ...

The Living Bible paraphrases it this way: "You went along with the crowd and were just like all the others, full of sin, obeying Satan, the mighty prince of the power of the air, who is at work right now in the hearts of those who are against the Lord."

   a. Because of our former tendency to sin, what severe indictment does Ephesians 2:3b make against us?

What a hopeless and helpless state we were in because of sin. From the first few verses in this chapter, it would seem that all was lost. But the first two words of verse 4 bring new hope.

   b. What are they?

Ray C. Stedman calls these words, "The first two notes of a glorious symphony."

3. Verse 4 tells us two important things about our God. What are they?

LESSON TWO

What a high and holy passage of Scripture this is! In it we see: 1) ourselves—dead to God because of sin and, 2) God—the all-merciful one.

Ironside says of God's mercy that there are, "Infinite resources of mercy for the vilest sinner … There is no one for whom there is no mercy."

Sometimes we are led to think otherwise. For example: What about the people in the farthest regions of the world who can't hear the gospel message?

4. What does it do for you to know that there is no one for whom there is no mercy?

   a. With God's mercy in mind, what encouragement do we gain in Hebrews 4:16?

5. What three things did this merciful loving God do for us? vv. 5-6

   1.
   2.
   3.

This completes the structure of the long sentence that makes up verses 1-7. God is the subject. These are the three main verbs: *made alive* with, *raised up* with, *seated* with. The object of all this is us!

   a. Why did He do all this? v. 7

You and I are the demonstration of the riches of God's grace. The Living Bible says it this way, "And now God can always point to us as examples of how very, very rich His kindness is, as shown in all He has done for us through Jesus Christ."

Stone of Remembrance:

"For we are His workmanship, created in Christ Jesus for good works, which God prepared beforehand, that we should walk in them." Ephesians 2:10

Day 2
Daily Facts
Read Ephesians 2:8-10

Saved by grace!
Ephesians 2:8-9 takes us right back to verses 4-5 and what we have already learned in this chapter so far—we were dead in our sins, but God, being rich in mercy, made us alive together with Christ!

1. According to verse 8, in a word, by what are we saved?

    a. Whose grace?

    b. See if you can define the word grace.

2. Was this grace in response to anything we did or did not do in the way of good works?

    a. How does Titus 3:5 confirm this?

LESSON TWO

    b. How does Ephesians 2:5 prove the point that we are saved totally by God's grace?

3. The grace by which we are saved is God's. Who paid the actual price for our sin? 1 Corinthians 15:3-4

This acronym of grace has been given:

G—God's
R—riches
A—at
C—Christ's
E—expense

    a. Romans 5:6 may give the most beautiful picture of God's grace to us in Christ. What does it say?

4. Verse 8 tells us we have been saved by grace through … what?

    a. According to this verse, where did we get the faith to believe?

    b. Is there anything in our salvation that we can boast about or take pride in? Why?

    c. Do you ever find yourself thinking more highly of yourself because you have become a Christian? Does this verse help you see this from another perspective? Instead of thinking more highly of yourself—what should be your response to unbelievers?

Notice this verse says we are saved by grace (the grace of God) through faith.

    d. Where does Romans 10:17 say we get this faith?

We don't need to muster up the faith to believe that we are saved. It is not *our* faith that saves us—it is God who saves us. If we have believed that Jesus is the Savior and asked Him to forgive us our sins and to save us from judgment—then He has! The enemy loves to keep people in question over whether or not they are really saved. If this is a problem for you—write out the words of Ephesians 2:8 and put them up somewhere you can see them often!

5. Verse 10 speaks to us about our own creation:

✢ How were we created?

✢ Why were we created?

The word *workmanship* is the Greek word poiema. It means work of art or masterpiece. It is the word for which we get our word poem.

    a. This verse tells you that you are His workmanship—His poem—His masterpiece! That is the way He sees it! The world is always talking about our self-image. What does this verse do for your self-image?

6. Who has already prepared your good works for you? What do you think this means?

LESSON TWO

a. How does the fact that you are His work of art, or specific creation, factor into the fact that He has prepared the works you will do?

b. Since God has already prepared your good works—what, according to verse 10, is your part? Share your thoughts on what this means. You may wish to see John 15:4-5.

Review this week's memory verse.

Day 3
Daily Facts

Read Ephesians 2:11-22

Unified!
This chapter begins great and continues to be great. We saw what we are and what God has done for us individually through the cross of Christ, and now we step back a little and look at this whole work of redemption from a bigger perspective—the perspective of Jews and Gentiles. Remember Paul is a Jew writing to Gentiles.

1. In verse 11, Paul immediately makes note of that which marks the greatest physical distinction between the Jew and the Gentile. What is that?

The mark of circumcision was that which physically separated Jews from Gentiles. It was the mark of the covenant of God with His chosen people. And yet, Paul says, it is performed in the flesh by human hands.

In other words, it may be a sign of the covenant with God, but it is still a physical mark, unable to touch the spirit or impart life.

2. In verse 12, Paul paints a picture of the Gentile's standing in regard to God, which is in direct contrast to the Jew's privileged position. He gives 5 points of separation. Fill in the one word that most describes the Gentile:

"Remember that you were at that time:
   1) _____ from Christ,
   2) _____ from the commonwealth of Israel, and
   3) _____ to the covenants of promise, having
   4) _____ _____ and
   5) _____ _____ in the world."

   a. This sad picture is the truth of the matter for the Gentile before Christ. Verse 13 says, "But now …" What happened that changed this tragic state of things?

3. Carefully read verses 14-16. Verse 14 tells us that Jesus Christ is our peace. See if you can share from these verses how it is that Jesus brought peace between the Jew and the Gentile.

Formerly there were Jews—chosen by and belonging to God and Gentiles—all those who were not part of the nation of Israel. The law brought enmity because it was through God's law that circumcision and other ordinances were established, physically separating the Jew from the Gentile. This separation caused strife—the Jew looking down on the Gentile because he didn't follow God's law and was not a part of His people.

LESSON TWO

When Jesus died on the cross, His life fulfilled the Old Testament law, and now we receive life and righteousness through belief in His atoning death. Now—instead of two groups, there is only one. Neither Jew nor Gentile—but a new man—a Christian!

    a. See what Galatians 3:28 says on this point.

4. What has been accomplished for both the Jew and the Gentile by Jesus' death on the cross?

verse 16

verse 18

    a. Look back at the description we had of the Gentile's relationship to God in verse 12. What is the Gentile's relationship now because of all that Jesus has done? v. 19

Paul has been giving us the picture of the two groups being made into one new man. Now he switches to the metaphor of a building—actually a temple.

5. According to verse 20, what is the foundation of the building?

This actually speaks of the testimony of the apostles and the prophets—the foundation that they laid of the gospel of Christ.

    a. 1 Corinthians 3:10-11 gives us a clearer understanding of the foundation of the church of Christ. What is this foundation?

    b. Who is the cornerstone, according to Ephesians 2:20?

The cornerstone was the most important part of the structure of a building. It not only had to be strong enough to support the building but every other part of the structure was lined up with it, and it held the whole structure together. In the east, it was considered to be even more important to the structure than the foundation. Often the royal name was inscribed on it!

Verse 21, speaking of Christ, says, "in whom the whole building being fitted together is growing into a holy temple in the Lord." In Christ—the foundation and cornerstone of the church, each individual Christian is being fitted together and growing into a holy temple—the Church.

6. Who will dwell in this holy temple? v. 22

In the Old Testament, God's glory was in the temple. In the New Testament, His glory is in the Church! Listen to what John MacArthur says as he concludes this portion of Scripture in his commentary: "Through the blood, the suffering flesh, the cross, and the death of the Lord Jesus Christ, aliens become citizens, strangers become family, idolaters become the temple of the true God, the hopeless inherit the promises of God, those without Christ become one in Christ, those far off are brought near, and the godless are reconciled to God. Therein is the reconciliation of men to God and of men to men."

Review this week's memory verse.

Day 4
Overview of Ephesians 2

Today we will be looking at the passage we have studied this week as a whole. The goal is to find the main lessons the Lord has for us from this chapter. Don't worry about being clever or profound—just do your best!

Find the Facts...

1. See if you can state the *content* of this week's passage in a couple of sentences. (Who is speaking, what is taking place, what is the main subject?)

Look for the Heart...

2. What do you think is the main *lesson* of this chapter? (What spiritual truths are taught here? Look for a command, a word of exhortation, a promise, etc.)

Hear Him Speak...

3. Look for a *personal application* from the content of this chapter. It should come from the lesson you got from the chapter (question 2). How will you apply the lesson to yourself?

4. Was there a particular verse that ministered to you this week? What was it and how did it minister to you?

5. Write out your stone of remembrance *from memory*!

EPHESIANS 3

Day 1
Daily Facts

Read Ephesians 3:1-6

In Ephesians 2, Paul revealed the great work of unity accomplished by Christ for the Jew and the Gentile. In chapter 3, he continues his thoughts beginning with the words, "For this reason ..." Because of what he has already shared—the revelation of the union of the Jew and the Gentile, Paul has in mind to offer a prayer in their behalf, but before he can get that far his thoughts take a momentary turn (as they often do!) and—much to our delight—he digresses on the subject of the mystery of Christ.

The mystery of Christ:
1. Compare verse 1 with verse 14. What similarity do you see?

It is commonly understood that what Paul began in verse 1 he began again in verse 14. Verses 2-13 form one of the eight long Greek sentences (in this case a parenthetical thought) that are unique to the epistle to the Ephesians.

    a. What does Paul call himself in verse 1?

    b. For whose sake is Paul in this state?

c. See if you can explain how it is that Paul's statement here is true: in other words, how is it that he is a prisoner for the sake of the Gentiles.

Verse 2 begins Paul's digression of thought. He has just stated his position as prisoner for the sake of the Gentiles, and from that very point he turns for a moment to consider the great mystery of Christ and his ministry to proclaim it.

2. Paul speaks of his ministry as a stewardship or an administration or a trust. According to verse 2, with what ministry was Paul entrusted?

   a. Paul says this stewardship was given to him for someone— who was that?

   b. According to verses 3-4, what was it that was made known to Paul?

3. Verse 6 defines the mystery in three parts. What are they?

   1.
   2.
   3.

   a. What does Galatians 3:29 show to be the prerequisite of being an heir of the promise in Christ?

   b. Do you belong to Christ? Does it matter at this point whether you are a Jew or a Gentile? What are you now, according to Galatians 3:29?

LESSON THREE

    c. What does 1 Corinthians 12:13 teach us on this subject?

This is the great message given by God to Paul to share with the world—the mystery of Christ, which is the equal status of the Gentile with the Jew. No longer separate from the promises fulfilled in Christ but fellow partakers of them all! No wonder Paul was willing to risk all to bring this great truth to light!

4. How is it that Paul was enabled to understand this mystery? (See verse 3.)

    a. From verse 5:

    ✛ Was this something that was previously made known?

    ✛ When was it made known?

    ✛ Who was the revealer of this mystery? (Not the apostles and the prophets—it was made known to them.)

The fact that the Gentiles would be blessed through the promises made to Abraham and that salvation would reach past the Jew to the Gentile was made known through the Scriptures in the Old Testament (see Genesis 12:3; Isaiah 49:6). But the full revelation of the equal status and position of believing Jews and Gentiles was a mystery—kept hidden until after the death and resurrection of Christ and only then revealed by the Holy Spirit of God.

This is the grace (unmerited favor) of God to the Gentile, of which Paul was made a steward or minister: "If indeed you have heard of the stewardship of God's grace which was given to me for you." To God be the glory. Amen!

Stone of Remembrance:

"Oh the depth of the riches both of the wisdom and knowledge of God! How unsearchable are His judgments and unfathomable His ways!" Romans 11:33

Day 2
Daily Facts
Read Ephesians 3:7-13

We remember that Paul began with the goal of offering a prayer for those he is so intently ministering to—but that, before he could get very far, his thoughts took him back again to the amazing mystery of Christ: equality for the Jew and the Gentile who had made themselves one with Christ. It was this very message of which Paul was made a minister.

The unfathomable riches of Christ:
1. Paul says in verse 7 that he was made a minister of this mystery by way of two things. What are they?

1.

2.

   a. Paul has been given an amazing ministry. He might have seen in it the occasion to think very highly of himself for having been given such a remarkable revelation. Did he? How does verse 7 give you the true picture?

   b. How does verse 8 add to the self-portrait that Paul paints?

LESSON THREE

2. From verse 3, we know that Paul had a revelation into the mystery of God's grace toward the Gentiles. In Galatians 1:12, we see how he received his understanding of the gospel. What does it say?

   a. 2 Corinthians 12 is an insightful passage describing another experience of Paul. Read verses 1-10 and share:

   ✣ What was Paul's experience? (vv. 1-4)

   ✣ What was the result of his experience? (v. 7)

   ✣ What was the truth that Paul brought out of this experience? (vv. 9-10)

Although Paul had an experience that was unmatched, and although he was given a ministry and message that were unmatched, yet Paul's weaknesses were ever before him. In 2 Corinthians 12:5, Paul says, "On behalf of such a man will I boast; but on my own behalf I will not boast, except in regard to my weaknesses."

   b. Do you find yourself boasting in the ministry you have been given or boasting in the things that have been revealed to you by the Holy Spirit? How might Paul be an example to you? Look back again at Ephesians 3:7. To whom does Paul give all praise and glory and credit for what he has been given? Is this something that you have learned to do?

3. In Ephesians 3:8–9 Paul gives two aspects of his ministry. What are they:

verse 8?

verse 9?

Paul says he was given the grace to preach the unfathomable riches of Christ. The word *unfathomable* means unsearchable, not tracked out, untraceable, past finding out. That is the depth and breadth and length and height of the infinite riches of Christ!

    a. Romans 11:33 speaks of the depth of the riches of the wisdom and knowledge of God. Read Romans 11:33-36, and share the conclusion Paul comes to about our great God.

Although it is Paul's ministry to proclaim the riches of Christ to the Gentiles, he himself says that they are past finding out. We will never fully know all there is to know about Christ, but we can certainly pursue Him and seek to know all that He will reveal.

Not only was Paul to preach the message of Christ's riches to the Gentiles, but he was to enlighten all men to the now revealed mystery of Christ—the equal standing of Jew and Gentile.

4. Ephesians 3:10 tells us what the result of the revelation of God's great plan would be. What does it say?

Every created being—whether evil or good—(this verse speaks in specific of the angelic world) would know the wonder of God's manifold (many colored, variegated) wisdom, love, and grace, as His eternal plan and purpose unfolded through the death and resurrection of Christ.

5. What was accomplished for you and me personally through Christ's work on the cross? v. 12

   a. Matthew 27:50-51 tells us what took place in the temple at the very moment that Jesus gave up His spirit. Read these verses and then read Hebrews 10:19-20 and share the significance of this event for you and for me.

Review this week's memory verse.

Day 3
Daily Facts
Read Ephesians 3:14-21

The love of Christ which surpasses knowledge:
Verse 14 brings us right back to where we started. The Amplified translates verse 14, "For this reason [seeing the greatness of this plan by which you are built up together in Christ], I bow my knees before the Father of our Lord Jesus Christ."

Because of all that Paul has been given to share with the Gentiles—the unfathomable riches of Christ—he bows his knees before his Father, and we are given the privilege of listening in on his prayer!

Some commentators say that there is really only one actual petition in this prayer—verse 16—and that the rest of the prayer is actually the results of that petition. Others say that it is a series of requests, one emanating from the other. We will look at it as one prayer with four petitions.

1. What is the first petition of Paul for the Ephesians? v. 16

The Amplified translates verse 16 this way: "May He grant you out of the rich treasury of His glory to be strengthened and reinforced with mighty power in the inner man by the [Holy] Spirit [Himself indwelling your innermost being and personality]."

   a. Do you feel a need personally for inner strength and reinforcement to live your daily life in this world? Where does this verse say this strength comes from?

   b. Look at Ephesians 1:19-20 (part of Paul's first prayer for the Ephesians), and share the extent of the greatness of God's power to us who believe.

   c. Is there anything in particular right now in your life in which you are struggling and weak? Name it right here and ask God to give you His strength and power to do that which will be glorifying to Him. And remember—the excellence of the power is of God, not of us!

2. What is the second petition of Paul for the Ephesians? v. 17a

The Amplified says it this way: "May Christ through your faith [actually] dwell (settle down, abide, make His permanent home) in your hearts!"

   a. Has Christ taken up permanent residence in your heart—or do you think of Him more as a visitor? Think about it this way: You may have asked Jesus to be your Savior, but have you allowed Him to be your Lord?

LESSON THREE

    b. What difference do you think it would make for your personally if you let Christ reign in your life?

3. What is the third petition of Paul for the Ephesians? vv. 17b-19a

The Amplified translates these verses, "May you be rooted deep in love and founded securely on love, that you may have the power and be strong to apprehend and grasp with all the saints [God's devoted people, the experience of that love] what is the breadth and length and height and depth [of it]; [that you may really come] to know [practically, through experience for yourselves] the love of Christ, which far surpasses mere knowledge [without experience] …"

The emphasis here seems to be on the practical experience of the love of Christ. Not just our head knowledge of His love, but our experience of His love.

    a. In what way have you personally experienced the love of Christ?

H.A. Ironside tells the story of a Spanish prisoner in an underground dungeon who left an impression cut into the rock of a cross, with the word above it in Spanish for height, the word below it for depth, the word on one side for length, and the word on the other for breadth.

4. What is the fourth petition of Paul for the Ephesians? v. 19b

The Amplified says it this way: "That you may be filled [through all your being] unto all the fullness of God [may have the richest measure of the divine Presence, and become a body wholly filled and flooded with God Himself]!"

Is this something you long for? It is Paul's prayer for you, and it is God's desire for you. In fact He commands that we be filled with His Spirit (Ephesians 5:18). You may pray this prayer with assurance of its answer!

5. Paul finishes this chapter with one of the most beloved doxologies in Scripture. What does verse 20 say that God is able to do for you?

It's as if Paul was not content to simply say that God was able to do all we ask Him to do—no, he says He will do *beyond* all we ask. In fact, He will do abundantly beyond all we ask—and even that is not enough: He will do exceeding abundantly beyond all we ask or even think! "To Him be glory in the church and in Christ Jesus throughout all generations forever and ever. Amen (so be it)."

Review this week's memory verse.

Day 4
Overview of Ephesians 3

Today we will be looking at the passage we have studied this week as a whole. The goal is to find the main lessons the Lord has for us from this chapter. Don't worry about being clever or profound—just do your best!

LESSON THREE

Find the Facts...

1. See if you can state the *content* of this week's passage in a couple of sentences. (Who is speaking, what is taking place, what is the main subject?)

Look for the Heart...

2. What do you think is the main *lesson* of this chapter? (What spiritual truths are taught here? Look for a command, a word of exhortation, a promise, etc.)

Hear Him Speak...

3. Look for a *personal application* from the content of this chapter. It should come from the lesson you got from the chapter (question 2). How will you apply the lesson to yourself?

4. Was there a particular verse that ministered to you this week? What was it and how did it minister to you?

5. Write out your stone of remembrance *from memory*!

EPHESIANS 4

Day 1
Daily Facts
Read Ephesians 4:1-6

Once again, Paul begins with a reference to what has already been said: "Therefore" (verse 1). Therefore, because of all that has gone before … "I entreat you …" We are now entering the second half of our study of the letter to the Ephesians—the repeated emphasis now becoming the believer's walk. Before you begin to study today, you may want to go back one more time and read those first three rich and blessed chapters of this letter, as they form the very basis from which the remainder of it will spring.

Keeping the unity:
1. Paul begins this half of his letter with a strong word of exhortation, really a challenge. What is his challenge?

The word Paul uses here, *entreat* (NASB), or *beseech* (NKJ), means "I appeal," and even stronger "I beg." Paul makes an appeal to those he has been speaking to, after telling them of all the riches that are theirs in Christ, he even begs them, now walk worthy of this high and holy calling.

a. Do you see why Paul would beg us to walk in a manner worthy of the all-gracious calling of God? What do you think it means to walk worthy of the call?

2. This desire to walk worthy of the calling was always uppermost in Paul's own mind and heart. He shares his testimony of this in Philippians 1:20: "My eager desire and hope being that I may never feel ashamed, but that now as ever I may do honor to Christ in my own person by fearless courage" (Moffatt).

   a. Why does it take fearless courage to live a life that is worthy of the calling?

   b. Paul desires that he will never feel ashamed when it comes to doing honor to Christ in his own body and life. We might realize that we sometimes do feel ashamed over living a life that is less than worthy. Here again Paul gives us the answer. What does he say in Philippians 3:13-14?

Paul's perspective in these verses is a continuation of the thought of unity. He has spoken very thoroughly in the last two chapters of the unity of the Jew and the Gentile in Christ. In chapter 4, Paul exhorts us to keep the unity, "being diligent to preserve the unity of the Spirit in the bond of peace," by walking worthy of the call.

3. The following is a list of four attitudes that will help to foster this unity that is ours in Christ. After each attitude given, share what you understand about the attitude and then share how this attitude will help foster unity in the body of Christ. v. 2

✚ humility:

✚ gentleness:

✚ patience (pertains in particular to circumstances):

✚ forbearance in love (pertains in particular to people):

4. Paul now gives us the basis for our unity—by way of the seven elements given in verses 4-6.

"There is …
    one _____
    one _____
    one _____
    one _____
    one _____
    one _____
    one _____

The point we can take from these verses is that the unity is ours in Christ. There is only one body—the invisible, universal church (to which all who are truly born-again belong), one Holy Spirit, one hope of our eternal future, one Lord—Jesus Christ, one body of truth in which we believe (have faith), one baptism (most commentators seem to think this speaks of water baptism) and one God and Father who is over all who are in Christ.

We don't have to create our unity or enhance it, or do anything else with it or to it. All we are asked to do is to preserve or, simply put, to keep it. We will do that as we walk in the humility, gentleness, patience, and forbearance that Paul has exhorted us to in these verses. Walking in a manner worthy of the calling with which we have been called!

Stone of Remembrance:

"I, therefore ... entreat you to walk in a manner worthy of the calling with which you have been called." Ephesians 4:1

Day 2
Daily Facts
Read Ephesians 4:7-16

Gifting the church:
Paul has just been speaking of our unity, now he speaks of our diversity: not in doctrine or in any way with regard to our position in Christ but in our personal giftedness and usefulness in the body of Christ.

1. As you look carefully at these verses, what good news does Paul pass along to us immediately? (See v. 7 and 8b.)

2. 1 Corinthian 12 is a passage which really explains the subject of our spiritual gifts. We may notice, when we read verses 4-6, that even in the diversity or variety of our gifts, there is still unity. How is this stated in:

LESSON FOUR

verse 4?
verse 5?
verse 6?

a. Why are we told these gifts are given? 1 Corinthians 12:7

b. How are they given? 1 Corinthians 12:11

In this 1 Corinthian passage, we are given a list of spiritual gifts (verses 8-10). You may read the list and make note of it for yourself. Another list of gifts is given in verses 28-30 of this same chapter and another list may be found in Romans 12:6-8.

In Ephesians 4:11, Paul gives another list of gifts—we might call them offices. What is interesting about these gifts is how Paul introduces them. He says, "And He (Christ) gave some as ..." It sounds as if he's speaking of people, not gifts. And this is what some commentators say about this chapter—that Paul is speaking of gifted *believers* given to the Church! What an interesting thought!

3. From this perspective, name the four gifted believers that Christ has given to the church as listed in this chapter. (You may list them as five if you prefer.)

   a. Ephesians 2:19-20 gives us a key to understanding the work of the apostles and the prophets mentioned here. What does it tell us?

   b. How does 1 Corinthians 12:28 speak of these first two gifted men?

This verse doesn't speak from the perspective of these being the greatest gifts or gifted men but more from a chronological standpoint—the first gifted men given to the church being the apostles and prophets, through whose ministry the foundation of the church was laid. They were followed by men gifted as evangelists and pastor/teachers.

4. Paul goes on in this passage to tell us the purpose of the gifting of the church. Verse 12 sums up this purpose in 2 parts. Share them.

It's interesting that in this passage the purpose of the gifts are pointed toward the believer in Christ. Paul is saying that Christ has given gifted men to the church for the building up of the body of Christ. That Christians would be equipped for the work of the service (in other words, ministry, to the world and to the Church) and that Christians themselves would be brought to maturity.

    a. Do you see yourself as a recipient of this kind of training, as you attend church and Bible study and seek to grow in service and maturity? Do you consider using your spiritual gifts so that you can be a part of this great spiritual building project? Share your thoughts.

5. What is the goal of the building up of the body of Christ? v. 13

    a. What is the desired result of all this work? v. 14a

6. Is this a work that you need in your life? Are you mature? Or are you still like a child, tossed here and there by every different thing you hear? Read Hebrews 5:12-14. What hint does this passage (especially verse 14) give you as to why one might not be mature?

    a. What does it mean to *practice* something?

    b. Are you practicing righteousness? What difference do you think this would make to you in your spiritual maturity?

    c. In Ephesians 4:15, Paul gives us another clue to becoming mature. What is it, and how would this help to bring maturity?

Verse 16 gives the result of all the members in the body maturing in Christ and doing their part: "Under His direction, the whole body is fitted together perfectly. As each part does its own special work, it helps the other parts grow, so that the whole body is healthy and growing and full of love." (NLT)

Review this week's memory verse.

Day 3
Daily Facts
Read Ephesians 4:17-32

Walking worthy:
Now Paul brings us right back to the subject of our walk, with some very specific instructions.

1. Paul begins with a command. On behalf of whom is he speaking as he gives this command? v. 17

   a. What is the command?

   b. Describe some of what Paul is relating as he speaks of the futile thinking of the ungodly (the NLT says, "they are hopelessly confused"). vv. 18-19

   c. In Romans 1:21, Paul explains how the ungodly became so confused. What does he say?

   d. What insight into their self-perception does Paul give in Romans 1:22? Share an example of the truth of this statement from our world today.

2. What is Paul's word to the Christian in contrast to the mindset of the ungodly? v. 20

a. Because we have learned Christ, have heard His words and have been taught truth by Him, Paul says we are to have another mindset and a different walk. From these three verses, what are we to do?

verse 22

verse 23

verse 24

The Amplified translates verse 22 like this: "Strip off your former nature ... which characterized your former manner of life." It's as if Paul is telling us to have no mercy on our flesh! It is a call to put off and then to put on.

3. What does Romans 13:14 tell you that will help you in this endeavor?

   a. What do you think it means to make no provision for your flesh?

Paul's teaching now becomes very specific. It even becomes personal, as he gives five specific commands. The encouraging thing here is that he not only tells us what not to do, but he turns it around and suggests that which we should do in its place.

4. From each of the following verses, write the three things we are taught: the negative command, the positive command, and the reason for the positive command.

verse 25
    negative command:
    positive command:
    why?

verses 26-27 (this one is difficult—just do your best)
    negative command:
    positive command:
    why?

verse 28
    negative command:
    positive command:
    why?

verses 29-30
    negative command:
    positive command:
    why?

verses 31-32
    negative command:
    positive command:
    why?

    a. Is there a particular area that has been touched in these verses in which you have struggled or are struggling now? Do these verses help you get the right perspective on that area? Why not stop right now and ask God to forgive you for your sin (1 John 1:7), and commit to Him your desire and determination to walk in victory—in the "new self, which in the likeness of God has been created in righteousness and holiness of the truth!"

Review this week's memory verse.

LESSON FOUR

Day 4
Overview of Ephesians 4

Today we will be looking at the passage we have studied this week as a whole. The goal is to find the main lessons the Lord has for us from this chapter. Don't worry about being clever or profound—just do your best!

Find the Facts ...

1. See if you can state the *content* of this week's passage in a couple of sentences. (Who is speaking, what is taking place, what is the main subject?)

Look for the Heart ...

2. What do you think is the main *lesson* of this chapter? (What spiritual truths are taught here? Look for a command, a word of exhortation, a promise, etc.)

Hear Him Speak ...

3. Look for a *personal application* from the content of this chapter. It should come from the lesson you got from the chapter (question 2). How will you apply the lesson to yourself?

4. Was there a particular verse that ministered to you this week? What was it and how did it minister to you?

5. Write out your stone of remembrance *from memory*!

EPHESIANS 5

Day 1
Daily Facts
Read Ephesians 5:1-2

Imitate God:
We begin again with a "therefore." Paul again referring us back to the first three chapters of this letter where he laid the foundation of our privileges in Christ.

1. Therefore, because of all that God has done for us in Christ, what should we do? v. 1

    a. In Matthew 5:48, Jesus gives a very strong word in keeping with the essence of Paul's exhortation. What does He say?

This command was first given to Israel by Moses. The command given there was, "You shall be holy, for I the Lord your God am holy" (Leviticus 19:2).

   b. God says, "be holy," Jesus says, "be perfect," Paul says, "imitate God." How does Paul's exhortation help you to see how to fulfill God's command to Israel and Jesus' command to us?

Paul wants us to get the picture in our minds of the natural behavior of a child imitating their parent.

2. Romans 8:14 tells us that those who are led by the Spirit of God are indeed the sons of God. What do you learn in verses 15-16 of Romans 8? Is this true for you? Why or why not?

   a. 1 John 3 speaks to us on this same subject. What do these verses say?

   verse 1

   verse 2

   verse 3

   b. Romans 12:2 gives us some very important direction in our endeavor toward purity. What does it say?

   c. Are you imitating God or are you imitating the world? (Be honest!) Could it be said of you that you are purifying yourself, just as He is pure? Are you living a holy life? Are you attempting to the very best of your ability to be perfect, as your heavenly Father is perfect? If you cannot say yes, then what can you do to change the direction you are going? Be specific. (You don't need to share this—just commit it to God.)

3. In Ephesians 5:2a, Paul gives us the specific way to fulfill this command to imitate God. What does he say?

a. Who is our example in this? v. 2

   b. With what kind of love did Christ love us?

4. John again gives us good instruction on this point, also pointing to Jesus as his example. Look at 1 John 3:16-18 and share the heart of John's direction to us as believers.

   a. How does James add to this same exhortation? James 2:15-17

   b. Is this an area in which you need work? Have you loved in deed and truth recently? Have you ever loved this way? Is there anyone who may need a touch of sacrificial love from you right now?

5. Jesus not only encouraged us to walk in love, but He commanded us to. What does He say in John 13:34?

Notice—He is still our example!

   a. What will be one wonderful result of our fulfilling this great command? John 13:35

Stone of Remembrance:

"And do not be conformed to this world, but be transformed by the renewing of your mind, that you may prove what the will of God is." Romans 12:2

Day 2
Daily Facts
Read Ephesians 5:3-21

Do not be conformed:

1. Just as we are to imitate God by walking in love, Paul wants us to know what we aren't to do. Verse 3 names three prohibitions for the believer. What are they?

    a. Name some of the things that Paul would be referring to here. Be creative.

Paul says these things aren't even to be named or hinted at among the saints. 1 Thessalonians 5:22 KJV says that we are to abstain from even the appearance of evil.

    b. What might you need to do in your situation right now to abstain from even the appearance of evil in the way of immorality, impurity, or greed?

2. In verse 4, Paul gives three more prohibitions for the Christian. Name them.

    a. Give some examples of the kinds of things Paul is speaking of here.

    b. Are you guilty of any of these? How does Paul exhort you to use your mouth instead?

3. Verses 5 and 6 give the reason for Paul's strong words of exhortation. Share the important message from each:

   verse 5

   verse 6

Is this something you needed to hear? Although we know that every sin is forgivable, we must not fail to take Paul's words here to heart. The one who *habitually* practices immorality or impurity is unlikely a true believer in Christ.

   a. What does 1 Corinthians 6:9-10 say on this subject?

   b. Read 1 Corinthians 6:11. How does this verse help you understand why a true believer in Christ would no longer want to be a part of the things Paul has mentioned in these verses?

   c. What does 2 Corinthians 5:17 tell you about the one who is truly saved?

   d. If, as you are doing this lesson, you have come to question your own salvation, remember that God is only a prayer away. Turn to Him now and confess to Him your sin. Ask Him to come into your life and to make you a new creature in Christ. Trust Him to cleanse you of your sin and create in you a new heart. Share your new faith with your leader or another Christian friend so she can rejoice with you in your newfound faith!

4. What is Paul's exhortation in verse 7 (and 11)?

   a. What is his reason? v. 8

   b. According to verse 11, rather than participating in deeds of darkness, what should we do instead?

   c. Verse 13 describes how the deeds of darkness will be exposed. Read it carefully and see if you can explain. (Remember who the light is—v. 8.)

5. Verses 14-21 are a series of exhortations. Identify each one noted and share what it means to you.

   verse 14
   (a paraphrase of verse 14 could be, "realize your need!"):

   verses 15-16:

   verse 17
   (This ties in with verse 10—a very important direction for those who would imitate God.):

   verse 18:

   verse 21:

LESSON FIVE

    a. Look over these exhortations and share the one that would make the greatest difference in your life right now.

Review this week's memory verse.

Day 3
Daily Facts
Read Ephesians 5:22-33

Submit:

1. What command does Paul give the wife in verse 22a?

    a. Notice in this verse—to whose husband is the wife to submit?

    b. Is this command qualified in any way by the husband's character, intelligence, attitude, spiritual condition, or any other consideration? What does this fact mean to you?

Beginning in verse 21, with the call to mutual submission, we see the importance our love and reverence for Christ has in regard to every relationship noted by Paul.

2. Look at the verses mentioned below and notice how devotion to Christ should affect that relationship (in other words, how is the wife to submit to her husband, how is the husband to love his wife, etc.):

5:22b—wives

5:25—husbands

6:1—children

6:4—fathers

6:5—slaves

6:9—masters

    a. Does looking at submission from the angle of devotion to the Lord give you a new perspective? Share.

3. Verses 23-24 give the reason that wives are to submit to their own husbands. What is that reason?

An accurate definition of the word submit here would be "place yourself under the authority of," or "willingly adapt and adjust yourself to the authority of ..."

    a. Do the words *willingly adapt* or *willing adjust* help to give you perspective on the subject of submitting? Share.

Although in verse 24 we are told that the wife is to submit to her husband in everything, there are exceptions to this rule. We are nowhere told that a wife must allow physical abuse or suffer violence. Nor is she told to submit to immoral demands. It is important to note that her primary duty is to submit to Christ. If there is ever a conflict in submitting to her husband and submitting to Christ, obedience to Christ must come first.

LESSON FIVE

We have already noted in verse 25 that husbands are to love their wives sacrificially, Christ's love for the church being their example. In this passage, Paul lifts marriage to the highest level possible—seeing it as an illustration of the relationship between Christ and the church.

4. How does Christ care for the church according to verse 26?

   a. What is His purpose for the church as given in verse 27?

5. How is the husband to love the wife according to verse 28?

   a. Verse 31 is a quote from Genesis 2:24. What profound truth does it tell us about the relationship of husband and wife?

   b. What does a person do for their own body? v. 29

   c. How does this illustrate the way the husband is to care for his wife?

Here again we see the husband's care of the wife—his own flesh—is a reflection of Christ's care of the church—His body. "The mystery is great; but I am speaking with reference to Christ and the church."

6. Verse 28 says, "He who loves his own wife loves himself." From a purely common sense point of view—how is it that a person who loves their spouse loves their self?

a. What is Paul's final word in verse 33:

to the husband?

to the wife?

b. Is this an area you need to work on? Share how you will begin today (one thing) to fulfill this command.

Verse 33 in the Amplified says, "However let each man of you [without exception] love his wife as [being in a sense] his very own self; and let the wife see that she respects and reverences her husband [that she notices him, prefers him, venerates, and esteems him; that she defers to him, praises him and loves and admires him exceedingly]."

Review this week's memory verse.

Day 4
Overview of Ephesians 5

Today we will be looking at the passage we have studied this week as a whole. The goal is to find the main lessons the Lord has for us from this chapter. Don't worry about being clever or profound—just do your best!

LESSON FIVE

Find the Facts ...

1. See if you can state the *content* of this week's passage in a couple of sentences. (Who is speaking, what is taking place, what is the main subject?)

Look for the Heart ...

2. What do you think is the main *lesson* of this chapter? (What spiritual truths are taught here? Look for a command, a word of exhortation, a promise, etc.)

Hear Him Speak ...

3. Look for a *personal application* from the content of this chapter. It should come from the lesson you got from the chapter (question 2). How will you apply the lesson to yourself?

4. Was there a particular verse that ministered to you this week? What was it and how did it minister to you?

5. Write out your stone of remembrance *from memory*!

EPHESIANS 6

Day 1
Daily Facts
Read Ephesians 6:1-9

Submissive relationships:
Much of our study last week was devoted to the subject of relationships—in particular the relationship of husbands and wives. Ephesians 5:21 set the stage for what we learned there, as well as what we will look at today regarding the relationship of parents and children, masters and slaves: "And be subject to one another in the fear of God!"

1. In verse 1, what command is given to children and why?

Before giving another word of explanation, Paul hits the mark—it is the right thing to do!

    a. What specific attitude are children (of any age) to have toward their parents? v. 2 What are some ways you can fulfill this command.

    b. What is the promise given for the one who obeys and honors his parents?

c. Verse 3 doesn't necessarily guarantee a long and peaceful life but rather it is a principle. How might it be that the obedient and respectful child would have well-being and live a comparatively long life?

2. What word of caution does Paul speak to the fathers? v. 4a

   a. What are some ways a parent might provoke a child to anger?

   b. What might be the consequences for the child who is treated in this way?

3. What, instead, is the father to do with his children? v. 4b

   a. The following verses give us some direction in fulfilling Paul's command: Deuteronomy 6:6-7, 11:19; Psalm 78:4; Proverbs 22:6

   b. If you are a parent, what are some of the things you either are doing or plan to begin doing to fulfill Paul's command here?

LESSON SIX

At the time Paul wrote this letter, it is estimated that half of the Roman Empire consisted of slaves and many of them were Christians. Paul's words here would be the rules of conduct for Christian slaves and masters. In verse 5, Paul calls slaves to be obedient to their master. The word Paul uses for obey is a military term that means to follow orders.

4. In verses 5-7, Paul goes on to describe the manner in which they were to follow orders:

   verse 5

   verse 6

   verse 7

   a. What is the motivation for the slave to submit from the heart to his master? v. 8

   b. If Paul's words here are a description of how a Christian employee should behave—how are you doing? Use this checklist as a guide:

   ✚ Do you follow the orders you are given?
   ✚ Do you show respect for your boss?
   ✚ Do you serve your boss with a sincere heart (or from your heart)?
   ✚ Are you kind to your boss as well as other employees?
   ✚ Are you a person of integrity in whatever you do in the workplace?
   ✚ Do you do your job as if it was Jesus Christ you were serving?

5. Paul begins his word to masters with an interesting exhortation. He says, "And, masters, do the same things to them." Obviously the master is not in a position to obey the slave. Look back to Ephesians 5:21 for the key to what Paul is saying here. What does it say?

   a. What specific prohibition does Paul give the master/employer and why? v. 9

   b. How might the employer (could this be you?) apply these principles in relationship to his employees?

Stone of Remembrance:
"Greater is He who is in you than he who is in the world." 1 John 4:4b

Day 2
Daily Facts
Read Ephesians 6:10-12

The unseen battle:
In verse 10, Paul comes to his final topic of instruction for the Ephesians. It looks for a moment as if he has taken an abrupt turn in a whole new direction—but looked at in the scope of the entire letter, it is really a natural progression from the wealth of the believer (chapters 1-3) to the walk of the believer (chapters 4-6:9) to the warfare of the believer (chapter 6:10-20). You see, everyone who enters into a relationship with Jesus Christ and commits themselves to walk worthy of Him, immediately becomes the enemy of Satan, the archenemy of God.

1. Paul begins by giving us the most important piece of information we can have concerning spiritual battle—where we are to look for our strength. What does he say? v. 10

For any who have experienced the struggle of spiritual warfare—this should be great news!

   a. Verse 11a tells us how we are to do this. What does it say? (This topic will be discussed in detail in our third day of study.)

2. Who is our enemy, according to verse 11?

   a. The Bible is full of vivid descriptions and specific names of this enemy of our soul. Beside each of the following verses, give the name he is called in that verse, or write a word or two describing an aspect of his character:

   Genesis 3:1
   John 8:44
   John 12:31
   2 Corinthians 4:4a
   2 Corinthians 11:14
   Ephesians 2:2
   1 Thessalonians 3:5
   1 Peter 5:8
   Revelation 12:9
   Revelation 12:10

   b. John 10:10a gives us a perfect understanding of Satan's plan against us. What is it?

c. For an understanding of the original state and fall of Satan, read Ezekiel 28:11-19 (where it is believed that the King of Tyre represents Satan) and Isaiah 14:12-15 (which is believed to be an account of his fall).

3. Who is our struggle <u>not</u> against according to verse 12? What does this mean?

   a. Who, besides Satan, is our struggle against? (v. 12)

These verses show us clearly that Satan is not alone in his attempt to overpower us; and that there is a whole army (with rank and order) of spiritual forces arrayed against us.

   b. When we realize this, it can be an overwhelming discovery. But the word of God gives us our victory chant. What are we told in 1 John 4:4b?

   c. This is a battle we can't lose! You see, the victory has already been won on the cross of Jesus Christ our Lord! Colossians 2:15 gives us the good news. What does it say?

4. How do these verses describe our posture or our role in this spiritual battle?

   verse 11

   verse 13

   verse 14

LESSON SIX

Although there is indeed a battle being waged, our battle against the enemy is not an effort on our part to take new ground, it is an effort to hold onto the position that is ours. In Christ, our spiritual ground has already been gained, as we discovered so beautifully in the first three chapters of this letter. Our battle is to lay claim to and hold onto what is already ours in Christ. The enemy will attempt to rob, steal, and destroy our sense of confidence in the position, power and inheritance we have in Christ.

    a. From either your own personal experience or your understanding of the devil's character—see if you can identify some of the ways he might undermine your confidence as a Christian.

    b. What insight in your attempt to stand firm against the schemes of the devil do these verses give you?

2 Corinthians 10:3-5

James 4:7

Review this week's memory verse.

Day 3
Daily Facts
Read Ephesians 6:13-24

Ready for war:
Paul begins this passage with the words: "Therefore, take up the full armor of God, that you may be able to resist in the evil day, and having done everything, to stand firm" (v.13). Any day might be the evil day—we can never predict when the enemy will attack, so we must be prepared every day. Paul lays out for us the proper uniform and equipment for our battle, or, as Warren Wiersbe puts it, *what to wear to the war.*

1. In verse 14a, we see the first piece of our spiritual uniform. What is it?

    a. Considering that our battle with Satan is predominantly fought in the mind, how will knowing the truth of the Word of God and standing on that truth give you strength in your battle with your enemy, the liar? (Philippians 4:8 may be of help.)

2. Name the second piece of our spiritual armor. v. 14b

The Amplified translation says, "having put on the breastplate of integrity and of moral rectitude and right standing with God."

    a. We are in right standing with God because of what Jesus did on the cross. What does 2 Corinthians 5:21 tell you about this?

LESSON SIX

    b. Although we stand in the righteousness of Christ—we are also called on to live righteous lives. How will living a life of integrity and keeping a clear conscience help you face the enemy without fear?

3. From verse 15, name the third piece of our armor.

    a. Romans 5:1 helps us understand how we have peace through the gospel of Jesus Christ. What does it say?

    b. What wonderful news does Romans 8:1 give the one who has received Christ?

Our adversary would love to keep us in fear and condemnation, but we can stand in readiness, prepared for the attack by understanding and claiming the peace that is ours in the gospel of Christ. There is therefore now no condemnation!

4. What is the fourth piece of equipment we must have for the battle? v. 16a

    a. What are we able to do with this shield?

    b. Name some of the fiery darts the devil might throw at you to undermine your position in Christ.

    c. See if you can describe how faith can extinguish those fiery darts.

5. Verse 17a gives us our fifth piece of equipment.

   a. One of the devil's most disturbing attacks is in tempting us to believe that we have lost or will lose our salvation. Read Romans 8:30 and list the progression from predestined to glorified.

If you have received Jesus Christ as your Savior, then you can know for certain that you are in the process that is pictured in Romans 8—with the assurance of heaven as your final destination!

6. Name the final piece of equipment given in verse 17b.

Note: The sword of the Spirit is the only offensive weapon in our arsenal.

In Matthew 4:1-11 we see Jesus Christ use the Word of God to defeat the attacks of Satan. Read these verses, and notice that in each case His words were, "It is written."

   a. God's Word is full of promises that are yours to believe and claim if you are a Christian. See if you can explain how studying and memorizing God's Word will make you stronger and more able to resist the lies of the enemy.

7. Immediately after listing our spiritual armor, Paul gives us the piece de resistance—the final complement to the full armor of God. Warren Wiersbe calls this "the energy that enables us to wear the armor and wield the sword." What is it? v. 18

LESSON SIX

The Amplified says it this way, "Pray at all times (on every occasion, in every season) in the Spirit, with all (manner of) prayer and entreaty. To that end keep alert and watch with strong purpose and perseverance, interceding in behalf of all the saints (God's consecrated people). And pray also for me." (vv. 18-19)

    a. Remember again, from verse 10, in whose power are we to fight?

    b. Share how you will use prayer to fight against your adversary the devil.

Review this week's memory verse.

Day 4
Overview of Ephesians 6

Today we will be looking at the passage we have studied this week as a whole. The goal is to find the main lessons the Lord has for us from this chapter. Don't worry about being clever or profound—just do your best!

Find the Facts...

1. See if you can state the *content* of this week's passage in a couple of sentences. (Who is speaking, what is taking place, what is the main subject?)

Look for the Heart...

2. What do you think is the main *lesson* of this chapter? (What spiritual truths are taught here? Look for a command, a word of exhortation, a promise, etc.)

Hear Him Speak...

3. Look for a *personal application* from the content of this chapter. It should come from the lesson you got from the chapter (question 2). How will you apply the lesson to yourself?

4. Was there a particular verse that ministered to you this week? What was it and how did it minister to you?

5. Write out your stone of remembrance *from memory*!

ABOUT THE AUTHOR

Linda has dedicated her life to serving the Lord as a teacher, writer, and speaker. While teaching the Word of God, training leaders, and speaking at retreats and other women's ministry functions, she has also written curriculum for over 20 books of the Bible.

If you would be interested in having more information about her ministry, please visit her blog at www.lindaoborne.wordpress.com, or email her at myutmost1@aol.com.

www.ingramcontent.com/pod-product-compliance
Lightning Source LLC
Chambersburg PA
CBHW071409040426
42444CB00009B/2169